GRAPHING FOOD AND NUTRITION

Isabel Thomas

Chicago, Illinois

Edited by Nancy Dickmann and Rachel Howells
Designed by Victoria Bevan and Geoff Ward
Original illustrations© Pearson Education Ltd
Illustrations by Geoff Ward
Picture research by Hannah Taylor

Originated by Modern Age
Printed and bound in China by Leo Paper Group

13 12 11 10 09
10 9 8 7 6 5 4 3 2 1

**Library of Congress Cataloging-in-Publication
Data**
Thomas, Isabel, 1980-
  Graphing food and nutrition / Isabel Thomas.
    p. cm. -- (Real world data)
  Includes bibliographical references and index.
  ISBN 978-1-4329-1522-3 (hbk.) -- ISBN 978-
1-4329-1537-7 (pbk.) 1. Nutrition--Juvenile
literature. 2. Food--Juvenile literature. I. Title.
  TX355.T4526 2008
  612.3--dc22
                                        2008008460

Acknowledgments
The publishers would like to thank the following
for permission to reproduce photographs:
©Corbis pp. **8** (Lester V. Bergman), **12** (Mango
Productions), **14** (Neville Elder), **20** (Pablo
Corral V); ©Photolibrary pp. **6 left**, **22** (Fresh
Food Images), **6 right**, **25** (Foodpix), **18** (Flirt
Collection); ©Science Photo Library pp. **4** (Bjorn
Svensson), **16** (BSIP); ©Still Pictures p. **26**
(Readfoto/sinopictures), ©USDA Center for
Nutrition Policy and Promotion p. **10**.

Cover photograph of fresh fruits, vegetables, pasta,
cheese, and olives, reproduced with permission
of ©Getty Images (Alan Richardson).

Every effort has been made to contact copyright
holders of any material reproduced in this book.
Any omissions will be rectified in subsequent
printings if notice is given to the publishers.

The publishers would like to thank Harold Pratt
for his assistance in the preparation of this book.

Disclaimer
All the Internet addresses (URLs) given in
this book were valid at time of going to press.
However, due to the dynamic nature of the
Internet, some addresses may have changed, or
sites may have changed or ceased to exist since
publication. While the author and publishers
regret any inconvenience this may cause readers,
no responsibility for any such changes can be
accepted by either the author or the publishers.
It is recommended that adults supervise children
on the Internet.

CONTENTS

Some words are printed in bold, **like this**. You can find out what they mean by looking in the glossary, on page 30.

FOOD FOR THOUGHT

All living things need food. Green plants capture the energy in sunlight to make their own food. Animals, including humans, eat plants or other animals. Food provides energy to move and keep warm. It contains substances our bodies need to grow and repair themselves. Giving your body things it needs is called **nutrition**.

The collection of things we eat and drink each day is called our **diet**. Diets vary because different types and amounts of food are available. For example, anteaters live on a diet of ants, eating up to 30,000 every day! Humans are lucky—we can eat a huge variety of foods made from plants and animals.

How much do you know about the food you eat? There is a lot to find out. How does food help your body? How much energy does it give you? Where does it come from? Who produced it? All this information is called **data**.

Markets sell an amazing variety of foods for us to eat.

Pictograms

One way to collect data (information) is by asking questions. This is called a **survey**. For example, you could take a survey of your class's favorite foods. Drawing a graph makes the data easier to understand. It turns the information into a picture, making patterns easier to see. The data is sorted into groups. Each group is counted, and a pictogram is drawn. Each icon (picture) represents a different food. To find out how many there are, you can count the pictures or you can read the number on the **y-axis**. This is quicker than counting. You can see that the most popular food in this class is pizza.

Food	Number of students
Strawberries	3
Ice cream	5
Grapes	2
Pizza	8
Chocolate	6
Pasta	6

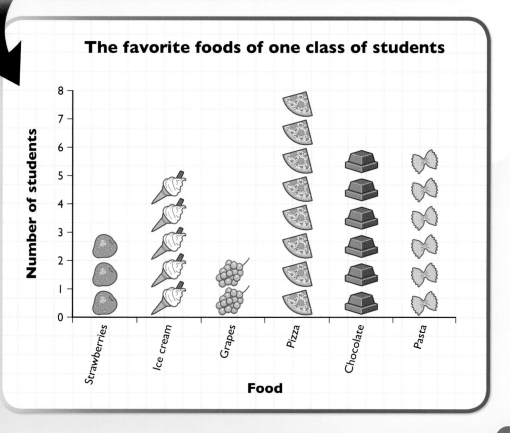

The favorite foods of one class of students

"YOU ARE WHAT YOU EAT"

If you lived in a different country, your school lunch might be very different. In Israel you might eat pita bread and **hummus**, and in Mexico you could have fried tortilla chips with salsa and cheese. Students in Norway often have bread with cheese or salami, yogurt, and fruit. Lunch in Ukraine might be beetroot soup with sausage and mashed potatoes.

People around the world eat thousands of different foods. It would be impossible to count them all. We can make **data** (information) about food easier to understand by sorting it into groups. Every food in the world can be put in one or more of these groups: grains, vegetables, fruits, milk products, **proteins**, oily foods/fish, **fats**, and sugars.

Which food do you most often have in your own lunch?

Bar charts

Students in a class counted the different types of food in their lunches. The data was recorded (written down) in a table using tallying. One tally mark was made for each food counted. When the marks are counted, the data can be turned into a bar chart. The **y-axis** shows the number, from 0 to 30. The **x-axis** shows the different types of food. Each axis of a graph must be labeled, to help people understand it. Drinks and food made from grains have the highest bars, which means that they were in the most lunch boxes.

Food type	Tally	Frequency (how many students)
Food made from potatoes and from grains, such as bread, pasta, rice, cereals, and tortillas	ЖЖ ЖЖ ЖЖ ЖЖ ЖЖ I	26
Vegetables or vegetable juice	IIII	4
Fruits or fruit juice	ЖЖ ЖЖ	10
Milk or foods made from milk, such as cheese and yogurt	ЖЖ ЖЖ IIII	14
Meat, fish, beans, and eggs	ЖЖ ЖЖ III	13
Oily foods such as nuts, avocado, and some fish	II	2
Fatty or sugary foods and drinks	ЖЖ ЖЖ ЖЖ	15
Drinks	ЖЖ ЖЖ ЖЖ ЖЖ ЖЖ II	27

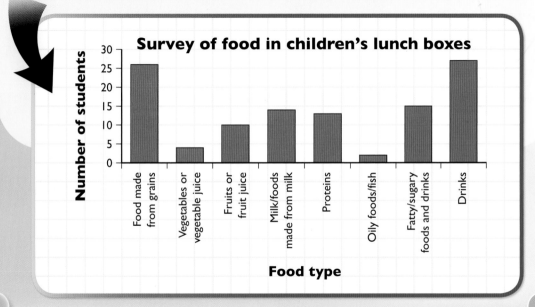

Survey of food in children's lunch boxes

A Healthy Diet

Humans need to eat foods from every group to stay healthy. Each type of food helps your body in a special way.

Starchy and sugary foods and **fats** are fuel for your body. They provide energy for walking, talking, playing, thinking, and everything else you do. Some of the energy in these foods is changed into heat to keep you warm.

Foods such as meat, fish, beans, and cheese are packed with **proteins**. Many parts of your body are made from proteins, and it uses new proteins from food to grow and repair itself. So, you really are made out of what you eat!

Fiber (the parts of plants that humans cannot digest) keeps food moving through your body. It is found in fruits, vegetables, and cereals.

Fruits and vegetables are also full of **vitamins**—chemicals that help your body to work. Dairy foods and meat are good sources of **minerals**, which are also essential for healthy **cells**.

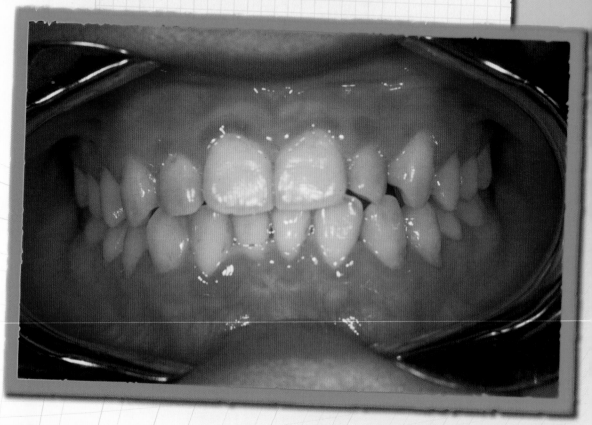

Scurvy makes people tired and weak. They often have swollen gums and loose teeth.

Getting enough vitamins

In the age of sailing ships, sailors on long journeys often suffered from scurvy. Doctors at the time did not know about vitamins, but they found that fresh fruits and vegetables helped to prevent the disease scurvy. Today, we know that the sailors were not getting enough vitamin C.

Graphing vitamin C

We can use this bar chart to find out which fruits and vegetables would have been best to take on ships. It helps us to predict which would be the best fruits or vegetables to give someone at risk from scurvy. Remember, though, that a graph does not tell the whole story. Green chili peppers are high in vitamin C, but sailors would not enjoy eating them every day! Fruits such as mangoes and papaya would not stay fresh on a long voyage.

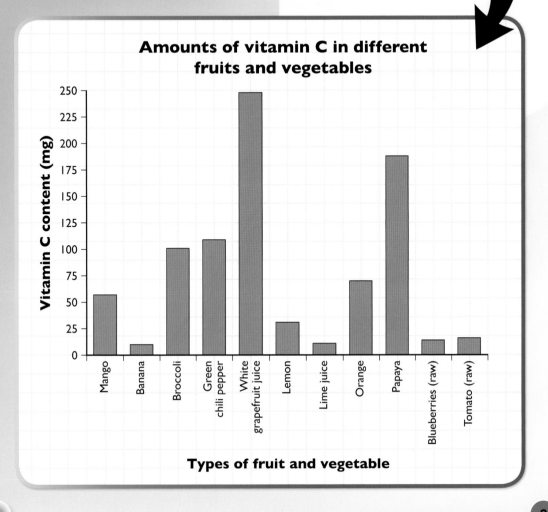

Amounts of vitamin C in different fruits and vegetables

GETTING THE BALANCE RIGHT

Your body needs more of some foods than others. Healthy eating does not mean cutting out all your favorite foods, but rather eating a variety of foods in the right **proportions**.

Starchy foods such as rice, bread, and pasta should be the main part of every meal. These energy foods contain **fiber** and **minerals** such as iron (for healthy blood) and calcium.

Vegetables are packed with **vitamins**. They are also good sources of fiber. Eat at least five different servings of vegetables or fruits every day.

Like vegetables, fruits contain lots of vitamins. They are good sources of fiber and natural sugars for energy. Eat at least five different servings of fruits or vegetables every day.

These foods are important sources of calcium, for healthy bones. They also contain **protein** and important vitamins. Try to eat three servings a day.

Foods in this group are the best source of protein, for growth and repair. They also contain vitamins and minerals for healthy **cells**. The oils found in some fish may help your heart to stay healthy.

Some types of oils are important for development and should be eaten in small amounts. These include the oils in fish and walnuts, and in vegetable oils and spreads.

PEACHES

FAT-FREE MILK

RAISINS

1% MILK

TUNA

GRAINS | VEGETABLES | FRUITS | MILK | MEAT & BEANS

Pie charts

A pie chart helps to show proportion. Proportion means how big a group of **data** is compared with other groups. A pie chart shows different groups of data as different sized "slices" of a circle. Imagine this circle shows all the food you eat in a day. The larger each slice of pie is, the more of that type of food you should eat. Make the portions on your plate match the proportions on the pie chart to make sure you are getting the right balance of foods.

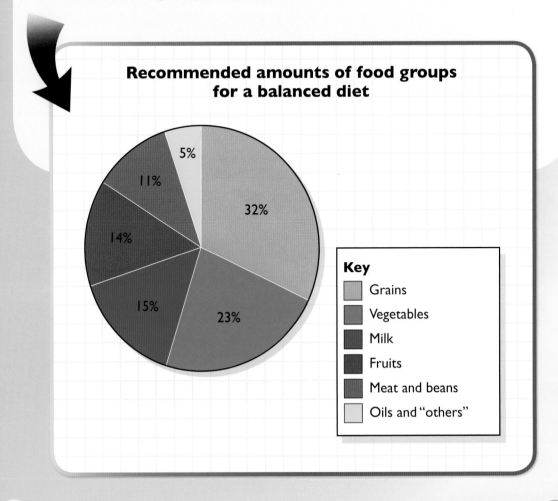

Recommended amounts of food groups for a balanced diet

Key	
	Grains
	Vegetables
	Milk
	Fruits
	Meat and beans
	Oils and "others"

All food contains stored energy. This energy is measured in calories. The more calories a food has, the more stored energy it contains.

Scientists burn food to find out how much stored energy it has. The energy is released as heat energy, which scientists can measure. Your body also burns food to release the energy stored in it. There are no flames when your body burns food, but some energy is converted to heat and movement, some is used as your body grows and repairs itself, and some is used to carry out tasks such as digestion.

How much energy do you need?

A 10-year-old boy uses around 2,000 calories and a girl uses around 1,750 calories (energy) per day just by being alive. Extra activities, such as sports or playing, use extra energy. Eating healthily means taking in only as much energy as you are going to use. For example, fatty and sugary foods such as cheese and chocolate provide much more energy than foods such as fruits and vegetables. If you eat too many fatty or sugary foods, you are likely to give your body more energy than it needs.

Riding a bike uses an extra 2 calories of energy a minute.

Graphing energy

The first bar graph shows how many calories (energy) are in different foods. To figure out how many calories are in your lunch, take a reading from the graph for each food you eat. For example, a cheese sandwich, a bag of potato chips, and an apple provides 440 calories. The second graph shows how much extra energy you burn every minute in different activities. Multiply each measurement by the number of minutes you spend doing it each day to find how many extra calories you burn in a day.

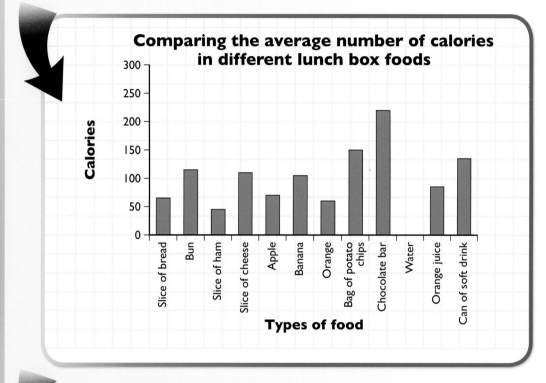

Comparing the average number of calories in different lunch box foods

Calories / Types of food

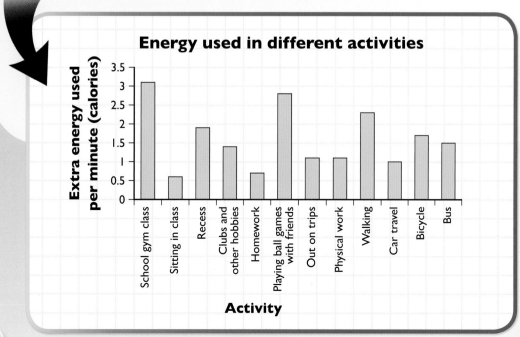

Energy used in different activities

Extra energy used per minute (calories) / Activity

When people eat more food than they need, their body stores the extra energy as **fat**. The first humans had to hunt or gather everything they ate. If they could not find food, stored body fat kept them alive for days or weeks.

Modern humans have a much more regular food supply, but our bodies still store extra energy as fat. More people than ever before are **overweight**, which means that they have too much body fat for their height. If nothing changes, almost 25 percent of U.S. children will be **obese** by 2020. Their extra body fat could cause health problems.

Losing weight

Eating too little is also dangerous for your body. If you do want to lose weight, always ask a doctor or nutritionist for advice. You will need to combine a balanced diet with fun and healthy activities, such as sports or playing outdoors.

In speed-eating competitions, people eat much more than their body needs.

Why are so many people overweight?

Most people become overweight or obese because they eat too many sugary, starchy, or fatty foods and get too little exercise. Portions of food are much bigger and provide more calories (energy) than they did 20 years ago.

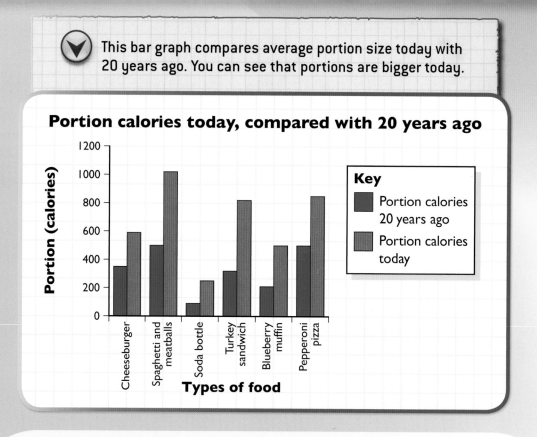

Portion calories today, compared with 20 years ago

Key
- Portion calories 20 years ago
- Portion calories today

Line graphs

More than 300 million people around the world are obese—and the problem is getting worse. A line graph is a good way to see how obesity **data** is changing over time. On a line graph, time is always shown on the **x-axis**. The **proportion** of the world's population that was obese in each year is plotted as a point. The points are joined together to make a line. The line rises up over time, showing that the proportion of people who are obese is rising.

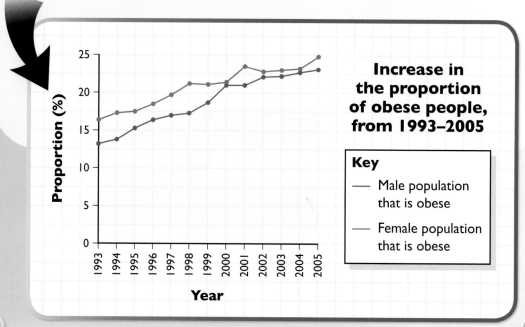

Increase in the proportion of obese people, from 1993–2005

Key
- Male population that is obese
- Female population that is obese

PLAQUE ATTACK!

Sugary foods have a second nasty effect: they can lead to **tooth decay**. This is bad news, because you need healthy teeth to bite and chew food!

Your mouth contains millions of tiny bacteria. These are tiny living things that feed on sugar in your food and drinks.

The bacteria form a sticky coating on the teeth called plaque. As they feed they make acids that attack tooth enamel (the hard top layer of teeth). If the acids stay in your mouth long enough, they make cavities (holes) in your teeth.

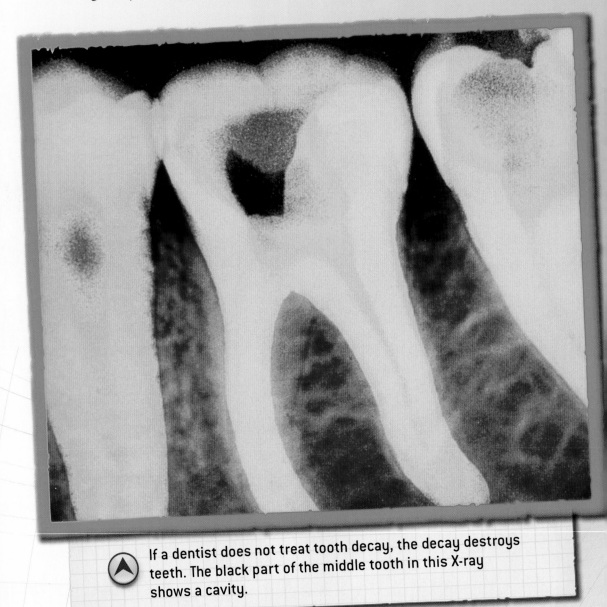

If a dentist does not treat tooth decay, the decay destroys teeth. The black part of the middle tooth in this X-ray shows a cavity.

Preventing tooth decay

Your adult teeth have to last for the rest of your life! Protect them by cutting down the time bacteria have to feed on sugars in your mouth.

- Brush your teeth and gums twice a day to get rid of sticky plaque.
- Eat fewer sugary foods.
- Don't eat after brushing your teeth at night.
- Only drink one portion of fruit juice a day. When fruit is crushed to make juice, all the sugars in the fruit are released. This is a sugary bath for bacteria.
- Avoid drinking soda. This is sugary and also contains acids.

Acid and tooth decay

This line graph shows the results of an experiment that measured how strong mouth acids were at different times after eating. Scientists measure the strength of acids using a scale from 1 to 7. Lower numbers mean stronger acids. Tooth decay starts when the line dips below 5.5 on the scale. This happens after 1.7 minutes. It takes 20 minutes for the mouth to get back to normal. If this person ate more candy after 20 minutes, the plaque would be acidic for longer.

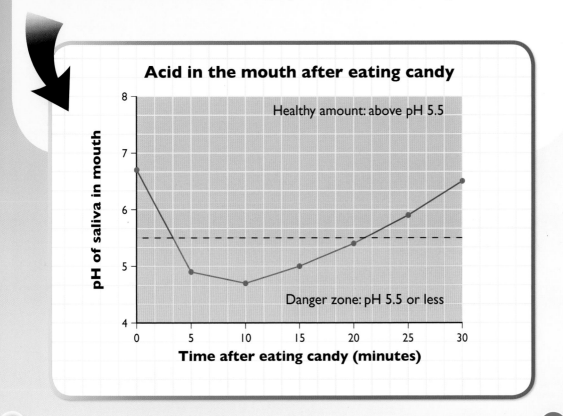

Acid in the mouth after eating candy

Healthy amount: above pH 5.5

Danger zone: pH 5.5 or less

pH of saliva in mouth

Time after eating candy (minutes)

WHERE DOES FOOD COME FROM?

The first time you see your food might be on a supermarket shelf. But before it was packaged, processed, and delivered to the store, it had to be grown or caught. Most of the world's food is produced on farms. Plants such as grains, fruits, and vegetables are grown on a huge scale. Livestock (animals such as cattle and pigs) are reared to produce meat and dairy products. Even fish can be farmed, rather than being caught from the wild.

Around the world, 1.5 billion cattle are reared for meat and milk. This is damaging the environment, producing 18 percent of the greenhouse gases that cause global warming.

To produce as much food as possible, chemicals are used to help crops grow. **Fertilizers** provide extra **nutrients** so plants grow faster or bigger. **Pesticides** kill insects or other living things that feed on crops. Some people worry that these chemicals are dangerous for other plants, animals, and people. **Organic** food is grown without using artificial chemicals. It may be better for you and kinder to the environment. However, it is more expensive to grow, so it often costs more.

Be your own farmer!

The best-tasting fruits and vegetables can be grown cheaply in your own garden. Try growing your own potatoes, lettuces, herbs, and tomatoes.

Double line graphs

Wheat is used to make foods such as bread, pasta, and cookies, and food for livestock. As the world's population grows, farmers must grow more wheat to feed it. This line graph has two lines. One shows the amount of wheat grown, and the other shows the amount of wheat eaten. (1 metric ton equals 1.1 tons.) Look at the places where the lines cross. In 2004 and 2005, the world produced more wheat than it used up. But since then, the world has used more wheat than it has produced. This means that stockpiles are being used up.

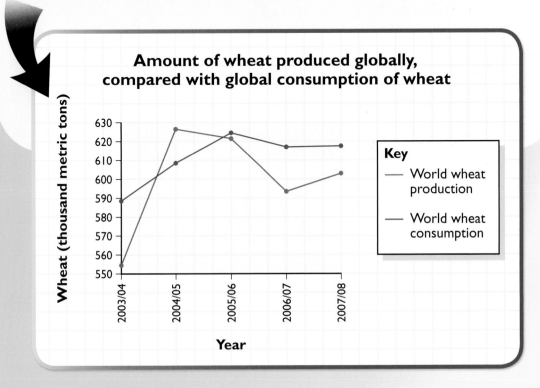

Amount of wheat produced globally, compared with global consumption of wheat

Wheat (thousand metric tons)

Year

Key
— World wheat production
— World wheat consumption

From the Farm to Your Plate

Different grains, fruits, and vegetables need different conditions before they will grow. Some need lots of sun and rain. Others need dry weather or a certain soil.

The climate of a country and the weather at different times of the year affect what can be produced. Tomatoes are only harvested in summer in northern parts of the United States. They are a **seasonal** food there. Many foods that we eat every day, such as bananas, do not grow much in the United States at all.

You can find bananas and tomatoes in a supermarket all year round. They are grown in other countries and **imported**. Even foods that can be grown in the United States are imported from countries where they can be grown more cheaply.

Bananas are always available in the United States, but they had to travel many miles to get there. This man is loading a cargo ship with boxes of bananas in Ecuador, in South America. They will travel a long way to reach their destination.

This map and table shows the "**food miles**" traveled by a typical lunch. Read food labels to find out where your food was produced. Use a map or an atlas to find out how many food miles it has traveled. Record the results in a table as you go along.

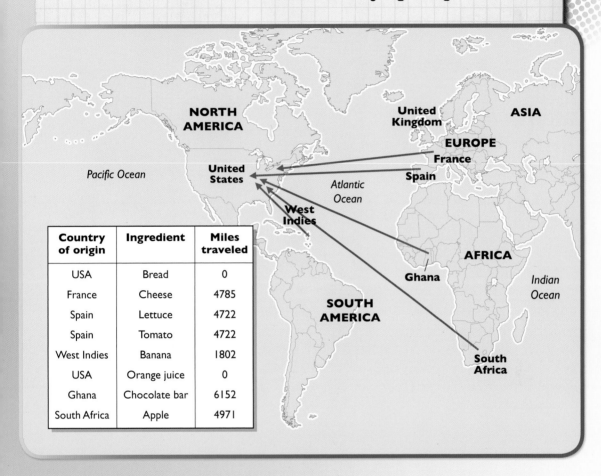

Country of origin	Ingredient	Miles traveled
USA	Bread	0
France	Cheese	4785
Spain	Lettuce	4722
Spain	Tomato	4722
West Indies	Banana	1802
USA	Orange juice	0
Ghana	Chocolate bar	6152
South Africa	Apple	4971

Food from far away

We can buy exotic foods from all around the world. This may seem like a good thing— but all the miles traveled on airplanes and ships can damage the environment and the food itself. From the moment fresh food is harvested, it starts to decompose (rot). The **vitamins** start to break down. The longer it takes fruits and vegetables to get to your plate, the less nutritious they are.

Foods that are produced locally (on a farm in your county) are usually fresher. You can find out about the methods used to produce them and even visit the farm where they were grown. If you shop at farmers' markets you can be sure that the farmer was paid a fair price.

READY TO EAT?

Some foods, such as tomatoes and apples, look just like they did on the farm. Other foods, such as grains, have to be processed (changed) before we eat them.

Food is processed for different reasons.

1 To make it edible. Wheat is crushed to make flour, which is mixed with other ingredients and then cooked to make bread. Raw wheat would be too tough to chew and digest.

2 To make it taste better. Raw cocoa beans taste very bitter. Combined with sugar and milk to make chocolate, they are delicious.

3 To make it safe. Milk from cows is heated gently to kill harmful bacteria.

Processing might just mean cooking or washing the food. Sometimes extra ingredients are added to make the food look or taste better and to keep it fresher for longer. Some of these **additives**, such as **vitamins** and **minerals**, are good for us. Others are human-made chemicals and may harm our bodies.

Much of our food is processed in places like factories, restaurants, or school kitchens.

Transfats

Transfats are oils that have been changed into solid **fats** by adding hydrogen. They are found in many processed foods, especially fast foods. Our bodies cannot digest them normally, and eating transfats has been linked with heart disease. Many food labels now warn you if they contain transfats—look out for the words "hydrogenated" or "partially hydrogenated" fats. In some countries, transfats have been banned.

Changing nutrients

Processing fruits and vegetables by peeling, cooking, or juicing them can destroy some of the **nutrients**. Some nutrients dissolve in water. When a fruit or vegetable is boiled, some of its nutrients "wash out" into the water. Then they are washed down the sink! This bar graph compares the vitamin C and iron levels after apples have been processed in different ways. It shows that it is important to eat some raw fruit.

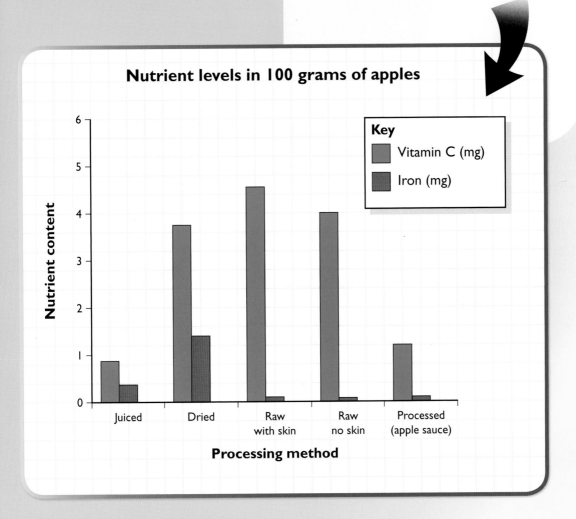

Nutrient levels in 100 grams of apples

Key
- Vitamin C (mg)
- Iron (mg)

Nutrient content vs. Processing method (Juiced, Dried, Raw with skin, Raw no skin, Processed (apple sauce))

BE A FOOD DATA DETECTIVE

Food labels list **data** to help you make choices about what you eat. Most food labels include a table of nutritional information.

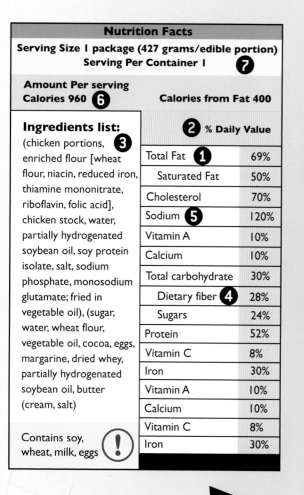

Nutrition Facts		
Serving Size 1 package (427 grams/edible portion) Serving Per Container 1 **7**		
Amount Per serving Calories 960 **6**	Calories from Fat 400	
Ingredients list:	**2** % Daily Value	
Total Fat **1**		69%
Saturated Fat		50%
Cholesterol		70%
Sodium **5**		120%
Vitamin A		10%
Calcium		10%
Total carbohydrate		30%
Dietary fiber **4**		28%
Sugars		24%
Protein		52%
Vitamin C		8%
Iron		30%
Vitamin A		10%
Calcium		10%
Vitamin C		8%
Iron		30%

Ingredients list: **3**
(chicken portions, enriched flour [wheat flour, niacin, reduced iron, thiamine mononitrate, riboflavin, folic acid], chicken stock, water, partially hydrogenated soybean oil, soy protein isolate, salt, sodium phosphate, monosodium glutamate; fried in vegetable oil), (sugar, water, wheat flour, vegetable oil, cocoa, eggs, margarine, dried whey, partially hydrogenated soybean oil, butter (cream, salt)

Contains soy, wheat, milk, eggs

1 Foods labeled "low **fat**" or "reduced fat" are not always more healthy. Reduced fat foods were often high in fat in the first place. Low fat foods may have extra sugar added, so the product provides the same total calories (energy).

2 These boxes show you how much **protein**, **carbohydrate**, and fat is in the product. It might show the amounts in 100 grams of the food, but the product may weigh more than that. If you eat more than 100 grams, you will be eating more of everything listed.

3 All ingredients have to be listed, including **additives**. Some of these chemicals are natural (such as ascorbic acid, which is vitamin C) and some are human-made (such as artificial colors and flavors). To avoid additives, buy fresh foods and cook the meal yourself.

4 **Fiber** keeps food moving through your body—you should eat around 12 grams a day.

5 Salt is often listed as sodium on a food label. It is important not to eat too much salt. You should have no more than 5 grams a day.

6 This information tells you how much energy is in the food. It shows energy in calories.

7 This is the manufacturer's suggested serving size, and it may be larger than a healthy portion.

Fast food

In the United States, fast food restaurants are increasingly being pressured to list the nutrition content of their food. This might help some people make healthier choices when they eat out.

Many people choose pre-made meals like this because they are quick and easy to serve. But they often contain high amounts of fat, salt, and calories. The best way to be sure your food is healthy is to cook it yourself.

Grains such as wheat, barley, corn, and rice are the main source of energy for most of the world's population. In 2007 the world produced over two billion tons of grain, enough to make over 40,000 loaves for every person in the world. However, more than 800 million people do not have enough to eat.

Food for all?

Some of the world's grain is used to feed animals or produce fuels. But the biggest problem is that food is not equally distributed around the world. Sometimes this is due to environmental problems. If **drought** makes crops fail, many countries cannot produce enough food to feed their populations. The other major problem is poverty. Although many countries produce more food than they need, poor countries cannot afford to buy this spare food.

 Drought may cause famine if people do not have the means to cope with water shortages.

Hunger is the world's biggest killer, claiming 25,000 lives every day. Even if people manage to get enough energy from food, they may not get the **vitamins**, **minerals**, and other **nutrients** the body needs to stay healthy. This is called malnutrition.

What you can do to help

In this country we are lucky to have an amazing choice of foods. Our choice of what to eat affects our health. Our choices also make an impact on the environment and on the lives of farmworkers in other countries. By learning more about the United States and the food you eat, you can make the right choices. For example, food that is labeled "Fairtrade" means the farmer was paid a fair price and will be able to feed his or her own family.

On this double bar graph, each country has two bars. One shows the percentage of the population living on less than one dollar a day, and one shows the percentage of children who are underweight. Can you see a link between poverty and malnutrition?

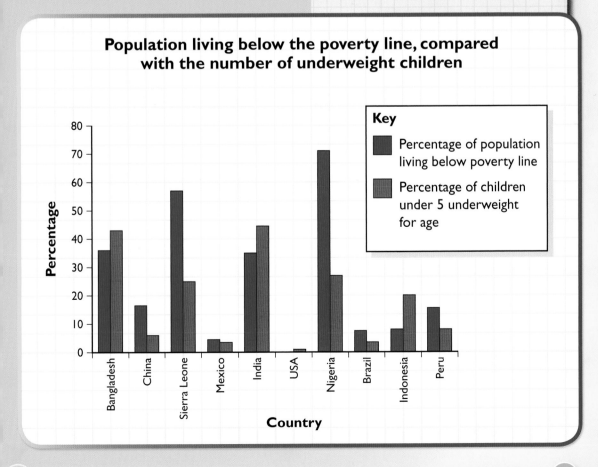

Population living below the poverty line, compared with the number of underweight children

Key
- Percentage of population living below poverty line
- Percentage of children under 5 underweight for age

Percentage (y-axis: 0, 10, 20, 30, 40, 50, 60, 70, 80)

Country (x-axis: Bangladesh, China, Sierra Leone, Mexico, India, USA, Nigeria, Brazil, Indonesia, Peru)

CHART SMARTS

Data is information about something. We often get important data as a mass of numbers, and it is difficult to make any sense of them. Graphs and charts are ways of displaying information visually. This helps us to see relationships and patterns in the data. Different types of graphs or charts are good for displaying different types of information.

Pictograms

Pictograms use pictures of things to show information. Each picture can stand for one unit or more than one unit. A key will tell you how to **interpret** the graph.

Bar graphs

Bar graphs are a good way to compare the data collected in a **survey** or an investigation. Bar charts have a **y-axis** (vertical axis) showing frequency and an **x-axis** (horizontal axis) showing the different types of information. When you are drawing graphs, always label each axis and give your graph a title.

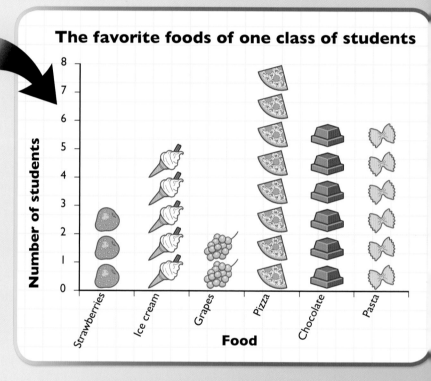

The favorite foods of one class of students

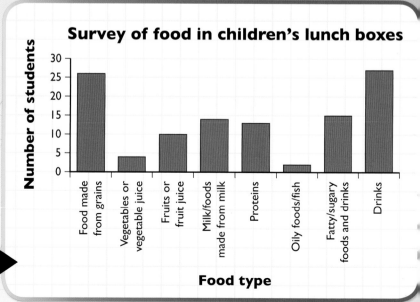

Survey of food in children's lunch boxes

Pie charts

Pie charts show information as different sized portions of a circle. They can help you compare **proportions**. When drawing a pie chart, you usually begin with the biggest portion at the "12 o'clock point" and then continue with the next sized portions in a clockwise order.

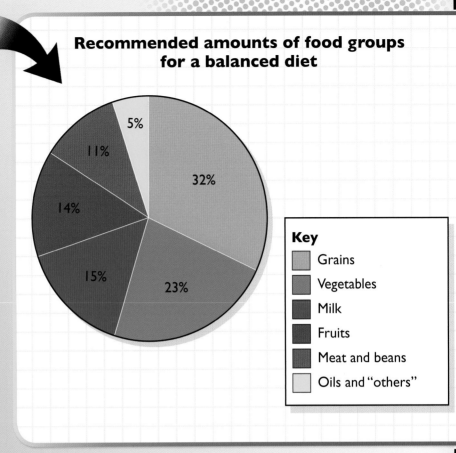

Recommended amounts of food groups for a balanced diet

Key
- Grains
- Vegetables
- Milk
- Fruits
- Meat and beans
- Oils and "others"

Line graphs

These graphs use lines to connect points on a graph. They can be used to show how data changes over time. Time is always shown on the x-axis. More than one line graph can be drawn on the same axes. This makes them easy to compare.

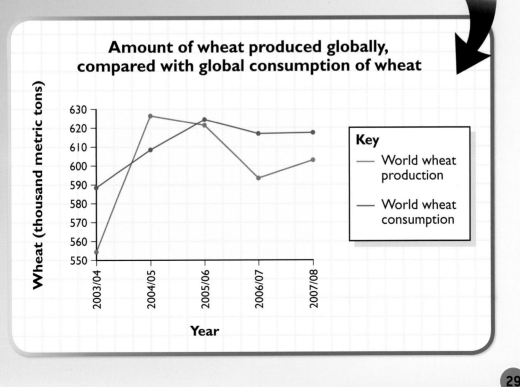

Amount of wheat produced globally, compared with global consumption of wheat

Key
- World wheat production
- World wheat consumption

GLOSSARY

additive chemical added to food to make it taste or look better, last longer, or be more healthy

carbohydrate nutrient in food that gives you energy

cell tiny building block that makes up our bodies and every living thing

data information, often in the form of numbers

diet collection of foods that a person or an animal eats. "Diet" is also used to mean an attempt to lose weight.

drought period of time when less rain falls than usual

fat group of substances that are found in foods and have a very high energy content. Also a layer of energy stored in the body.

fertilizer chemical added to soil to help crops grow bigger and faster

fiber parts of plants that your body cannot digest. Fiber helps food move through your body.

food miles number of miles a food product or its ingredients have traveled to get from the farm to your plate

hummus spread made from chick peas, olive oil, and garlic

imported brought into the country from another country

interpret use a graph to figure out the answers to questions about the data it shows

mineral substance found in foods that is important for healthy growth and development

nutrient substance in food that we need for health

nutrition giving your body the nutrients that it needs

obese very overweight

organic produced without using chemicals such as pesticides and fertilizer

overweight when a person is heavier than is healthy for his or her height

pesticide chemical sprayed onto crops to stop pests from eating or living on them

proportion size of a group of data compared to other groups or to the whole set of data

protein substance found in many foods that your body uses to grow and repair itself

seasonal food that is only available at certain times of the year in a particular country because it does not grow all year round

survey collecting information by asking questions

tooth decay rotting of the teeth caused by eating too many sugary foods

transfat solid fat that has been made artificially by adding hydrogen to oils

vitamin chemical found in foods that is essential for healthy growth and development

x-axis horizontal line on a graph

y-axis vertical line on a graph

Books

Bean, Anita. *Awesome Food for Active Kids: The ABCs of Eating for Energy and Health.* Alameda, Calif.: Hunter House, 2006.

Claybourne, Anna. *Healthy Eating: Diet and Nutrition.* Chicago: Heinemann Library, 2008.

McCarthy, Rose. *Food Labels: Using Nutrition Information to Create a Healthy Diet.* New York: Rosen, 2008.

Royston, Angela. *My Amazing Body: Staying Healthy.* Chicago: Raintree, 2004.

Websites

Play the MyPyramid Blast Off game, choosing the right food groups to fuel your rocket. This website is packed with information on healthy eating. www.mypyramid.gov/kids/index.html

The Kids' Health website offers suggestions for healthy serving sizes for kids. http://kidshealth.org/kid/stay_healthy/food/pyramid.html

The Farm Service Agency is a website with lots of fun facts about food. http://content.fsa.usda.gov/fsakids/food_facts.htm

Milk Matters is a website with information about calcium. www.nichd.nih.gov/milk/kids/kidsteens.cfm

Play games at the U.S. Department of Agriculture Food and Nutrition Service's website for kids. www.fns.usda.gov/eatsmartplayhardkids/

INDEX